PREFACE

Schumann's *Adventlied*, Op.71, too little known today, was composed in Dresden during November/December 1848 on a text by Friedrich Rückert. By his own account in a comment on 7 February 1848, Schumann noted down the text as No.48 in the handwritten collection of poems to be considered for composition that he and his wife Clara had begun in 1839. The copy, for what occasion can only be conjectured, was made in the midst of work on his opera *Genoveva*, Op.81. Possibly Schumann was looking for texts for new choral compositions of his own that he could perform with the *Verein für Chorgesang* he founded in Dresden in January 1848. The comment 'to treat it perhaps like a motet' under the title of the poem copy suggests that Schumann intended a sacred choral work. But it was not until nine months later that he began composing the work, on 25 November, the day he was first occupied with Rückert's *Makamen* and presumably transcribed the text for *Verzweifle nicht im Schmerzensthal*, Op.93, into the collection of poem copies. In the course of this he came across the copy of the *Adventlied* and was probably inspired to compose it. Schumann finished the work on 19 December 1848, recording this date at the end of the autograph score: 'Dresden, / 19 December 1848 / R. Schumann'.

Time and again there has been interest in Schumann's religiosity and his relationship to church music in conjunction with his choice of the *Adventlied* text on *Dein König kommt niedern Hüllen* which may still be found in German church hymnals. Here is a work that though religious was probably more politically motivated by current events, by the longing for peace and the revolutionary years 1848/49. Both works represent, according to Arnfried Edler

a peculiar, mixed genre between convivial, covertly political and religious song. With *Adventlied*, Op.71, [...] Schumann for the first time entered that curious

realm between e̶s̶t̶a̶b̶l̶i̶s̶h̶e̶d̶ to be explai of this age, a and gener

Rücke nated ca. 1 published in 1834 in the edition of the *Gesammelte Gedichte von Friedrich Rückert* by the publishing house of Carl Heyder in Erlangen. Between 1836 and 1840 there appeared four other issues, not identical to this edition,[2] in each of which the *Adventlied* was reprinted with an unaltered text. It was first included in a church hymnal in 1841 in Württemberg. Schumann's personal copy of the first edition of 1843,[3] as well as the edition of 1841 from the publishing house of Johann David Sauerländer are identical with the texts of the Heyder editions except for the orthographic difference in the sixth strophe, *Finsternis* instead of *Finsterniß*.[4] But since, according to an entry in his *Haushaltbuch*, Schumann first acquired this three-volume edition of the Rückert poems of the Johann David Sauerländer edition of 1843 on 31 May 1849, it is likewise disqualified as the basis of the text. It is therefore probable that the edition owned by the Schumann couple at the time of the copy was the second issue of the *Gesammelte Gedichte von Friedrich Rückert* from the publishing house of Carl Heyder, which Robert, according to the autograph comment on the flyleaf, had presented to his wife in 1837;[5] this served as source for the copy.

---

[1] Arnfried Edler, *Robert Schumann und seine Zeit* (Laaber, 1982), 228

[2] On account of the variable page numbers in the issues the *Adventlied* is found on different pages in each.

[3] Robert-Schumann-Haus Zwickau, Archives-No.: *6095, 1–C1/A4*

[4] Schumann also recorded *Finsterniß* in his copy of the poem.

[5] Robert-Schumann-Haus Zwickau, Archives-No.: *7901–C1/A4*. Schumann recorded on the flyleaf: 'Clara Schumann received this book as a present in the year 1837 from her then sweetheart Robert.'

In comparison with the supposed text source Schumann's copy shows several differences. He subsequently made three fundamental changes in the autograph score.[6]

On 17 March 1849 Schumann offered the *Adventlied* for publication to the publisher N.Simrock in Bonn. In his answer of 29 March, Simrock declared that he was in fact ready to print some of Schumann's compositions, but declined this work as well as the *Konzerstück für vier Hörner*, Op.86. Thereupon, already on 19 April Schumann contacted the publishers Breitkopf & Härtel about taking on publication of Op.71, which they accepted on 26 April. On 2 May Schumann dispatched the parts and piano reduction of the *Adventlied* to the publishing house.

At first the later title *Adventlied* going back to Rückert was not going to be retained. Concerning this Schumann wrote in the explanatory covering letter of the despatch to Hermann Härtel:

I do not want to call it 'Adventlied', as Rückert named it, because this is a reminder of a certain time of year and would limit the performance of the piece to a certain extent. 'Cantata' is a rather overused word – and so there remains for me nothing but the simple: Geistliches Gedicht [Sacred Poem], with which perhaps you, I hope, will be in agreement.[7]

Schumann, however, was subsequently persuaded by Hermann Härtel to give the work the title known today.

The printed vocal parts appeared in June 1849 – Schumann received them on 22 June – and the two-hand piano reduction in November 1849. The score was initially sold as a publishing-house copy, to which the comment 'The score can be obtained in clean copies from the publisher' on the printed piano score refers. It was first published posthumously in April 1866.

As early as two months after Schumann had finished composing the *Adventlied*, he rehearsed the work on 21 February in the *Verein für Chorgesang* he founded in 1848. Consequently, the vocal parts were copied from the autograph score. The *Adventlied* was also rehearsed in the meetings up to 17 April, about which Schumann's entries give information in his *Chornotizbuch*.[8] On 12 September he rehearsed the work in the Dresden choral union for the last time. But Julius Rietz in Leipzig was also interested in the piece and worked on it with the Leipzig *Singakademie* founded in 1802. Then on 10 December 1849 it was premiered under his direction in the *Konzert zum Besten der hiesigen Armen* ['Concert in Aid of the Local Poor'] in the Gewandhaus by the Leipzig *Singakademie* and the *Thomanerchor*.

It was first performed as early as in February 1850 in Schumann's birthplace Zwickau. Other performances mentioned on the flyleaf of his personal copy of the piano score took place on 24 October 1850 in Düsseldorf and on 12 May 1856 during the 24th Lower Rhine Music Festival under Julius Rietz.[9]

---

[6] All these differences have been listed in: *Robert Schumann. Neue Ausgabe sämtlicher Werke*, Series IV, Work Group 3, Vol.1, 2, ed. Ute Bär (now Scholz) (Mainz, 2011).

[7] Hessische Landes- und Hochschulbibliothek, Musikabteilung, Darmstadt; Breitkopf & Härtel Archiv; siglum: *Nr. 69*. The reprints in *Robert Schumanns Briefe. Neue Folge*, ed. F.Gustav Jansen (Leipzig, 1886), 372f. and *Briefe NF, 2/1904*, 460f. are incomplete.

[8] Robert Schumann-Haus Zwickau, Archives-No.: *4871 / VII,C, 6–A3*.

[9] Clara Schumann added this comment on the flyleaf of Schumann's personal copy.

Editorial Notes

Extant Music Sources

SK   Sketches of Op.71
Universitäts- und Landesbibliothek Bonn, siglum: *Schumann 6*
The sketches of the *Adventlied* originating between 25 and 30 November 1848 in Dresden were acquired in November 1911 by Oberbergrat [chief counsellor of mines] Dr h.c. Alfred Wiede, from C.G.Boerner in Leipzig, together with numerous other autographs not included in the catalogue. The MS belonged to the heirs of Alfred Wiede until 1974 when it was sold by the music antiquarian bookseller Hans Schneider, Tutzing, to the present owner institution.
The MS comprises three bifolios à 4 pages of the same paper type, each hand-ruled with 24 staves and successively notated in black-brown ink; the folios were originally bound with a red ribbon, presently unfastened.
The sketches contain mainly the vocal setting. For this Schumann, from the second page, left off notating in short-score form and up to the last page had written down the individual, though not always completely worked out vocal parts on each of the four-stave systems. The verbal text is completely present (if not always in all parts).

P   Autograph score of Op.71
Staatsbibliothek zu Berlin, Preußischer Kulturbesitz, Musikabteilung mit Mendelssohn-Archiv; siglum *Mus. ms. autogr. R. Schumann 8*
The autograph score originating between 3 and 19 December 1848 in Dresden and expanded prior to 22 October 1850 in Düsseldorf, which is bound together with the autographs *Mus. ms. autogr. R. Schumann 9* (Op.93) and *Mus. ms. autogr. R. Schumann 10* (Op.144), was offered for sale by Clara Schumann in 1887, together with others of Robert Schumann's MSS, to the Königliche Bibliothek Berlin. It has remained on deposit there since 1890. Financed by the Berlin publisher Dr Hermann Paetel, it passed into the possession of the present Staatsbibliothek zu Berlin – Preußischer Kulturbesitz.
The autograph score of the *Adventlied,* Op.71, comprises 72 pages. Preceding the music text is an unruled title-page, on whose recto page, centred, Schumann notated in dark brown ink the title of the work. The music text comprises 17 bifolios plus a single folio, each with 24 hand-ruled staves in light brown ink on which Schumann continuously notated the music text.

OS   Original edition of the vocal parts of Op.71
Leipzig, by Breitkopf & Härtel, June 1849
Title-page: *ADVENTLIED / von / Friedrich Rückert / für Sopran Solo und Chor / mit Begleitung des Orchesters / componirt / von / ROBERT SCHUMANN. / OP. 71. / Singstimmen. / Eigenthum der Verleger. / Leipzig, bei Breitkopf & Härtel. / Pr. 1 Thlr. / 7971. / Eingetragen in das Vereinsarchiv.*
OS comprises the parts for soprano (including the solo part), alto, tenor I, tenor II and bass. The interchange between solo and chorus was noted above each stave in the individual parts by *Solo* or *Chor,* respectively. With simultaneous entrances of solo and chorus the parts were engraved on two separate staves.

KA Original edition of the piano reduction of Op.71

Leipzig, by Breitkopf & Härtel, presumably between 16 September and 16 October 1849

Title-page: *Adventlied / von / Friedrich Rückert / für Sopran Solo und Chor / mit Begleitung des Orchesters / componirt / von / ROBERT SCHUMANN. / Op. 71. / Clavierauszug / VON R. PFRETZSCHNER. / Eigenthum der Verleger. / Leipzig, bei Breitkopf & Härtel. / Pr. 1 Thlr. 15 Ngr. / 7970. / Eingetragen in das Vereinsarchiv. / Die Partitur ist in saubern Abschriften von der Verlagshandlung zu beziehen.* ['The score can be obtained in clean copies from the publisher.']

The music text is on pp3–35. The verso pages of the title-page and the final music folio are blank.

HAD Manuscript performance parts of Op.71 for the *Städtische Musikverein Düsseldorf*

Heinrich-Heine-Institut Düsseldorf; *Depositum des Städtischen Musikvereins Düsseldorf*; siglum: *367.3*

The performing materials of the *Adventlied* prepared for the Düsseldorf *Musikverein* before 24 October 1850 and 12 May 1856 comprise in addition to printed vocal and string parts, 35 manuscript orchestral and 46 vocal parts. Most of the instrumental parts were written by Otto Hermann Klausnitz and prepared for the performance at the Lower Rhine Music Festival in 1856. In addition the bundle of papers contains five instrumental parts notated by A.Ottmann, that were probably prepared in conjunction with the Düsseldorf first performance of the work on 24 October 1850. Amongst those written by Ottmann are all three trombone parts with correc-

tions matching those in the autograph score, possibly contingent on performance conditions.

PA1–3 Copies 1–3 of the score of Op.71

PA1 Gesellschaft der Musikfreunde in Vienna; siglum: *28159*

PA2 Toonkunst-Bibliothek, Amsterdam; siglum: *Mus. Schum 2*

PA3 Toonkunst-Bibliothek, Amsterdam; siglum: *Mus. Schum 3*

After Schumann had returned to Breitkopf & Härtel on 2 December 1849 the corrected original copy of the model for the sales copies of the score, the piano reduction KA advertised on the title-page could be prepared and distributed. At this point in time Schumann had not yet added the trombone parts, so the corresponding copies could not have contained these.

The scores PA1 and PA2 written by various copyists each comprise 76 pages and show the same layout of bars and staves as well as the same title on the first music page above the first stave. Hence it is possible that they were copied from the same model.

The score copy PA3 clearly shows discrepancies from these two copies.

EST First edition of the four string parts of Op.71

Leipzig, by Breitkopf & Härtel, May 1856

Caption title: *ADVENTLIED / von / ROBERT SCHUMANN / Op. 71 / Leipzig bei Breitkopf & Härtel.*

Engraved below the caption title was the appropriate information for each part (Violino I., Violino II., Viola., Violoncello e Basso.). The plate number 9319 appears on each page of music. Noted on the first music page of the Vl. I part, bottom left, is the comment: 'Engraving and

printing by Breitkopf & Härtel in Leipzig.'
The parts of Vl. I, Vl. II and Vla. each comprise four music pages, that of Vc./Cb. comprises five music pages.

EP First edition of the score of Op.71 Leipzig, by Breitkopf & Härtel, April 1866
Title: *ADVENTLIED / von / ROBERT SCHUMANN / für Sopran Solo und Chor / mit Begleitung des Orchesters / componirt / von / ROBERT SCHUMANN / Op. 71. / PARTITUR. / Eigenthum der Verleger. / Leipzig, bei Breitkopf & Härtel. / Pr. 3 Thlr. 15 Ngr. / 10818. / Eingetragen in das Vereinsarchiv.*
The trombone parts are lacking in the posthumously published first edition of the score as well as in the extant score copies. Otherwise, just as with the score copies, it also shows no conceptual differences in comparison with the autograph score.

Evaluation of Sources and Edition

The genesis of the *Adventlied* is not fully documented by the extant documents authorized by the composer. Preserved on the one hand are the sources documenting the early stages of the text, on the other are the original editions of the vocal parts and piano reduction supervised by the composer that contain again variants in comparison with the autograph score, as well as the extant MS trombone parts used for the Düsseldorf first performance. Lost are all those sources documenting the textual stages between the autograph score and the original editions of the vocal parts and the piano reduction published in 1849. Belonging to these are the MS piano reduction produced by Robert Pfretzschner before 20 February 1849, the MS vocal parts finished before 21 February that Schumann used until the publication of the original edition and possibly still even beyond that in the Dresden choral union, together with the engraver's models and the galley proofs for the original editions of the vocal parts and the piano reduction. Not extant is, furthermore, the original copy checked by Schumann for the publishing house copies of the score that presumably served as the source for the likewise lost MS orchestral parts of the Leipzig premiere.

From this source situation it is clear that the respective main sources for the vocal parts and the piano reduction are their original editions and – since the four string parts were first available in print in May 1856 and the score in 1866 – for the orchestral parts, the autograph score. The original edition of the piano reduction served as comparison source for the vocal parts.

The orchestral part is published in the revised final version with trombones that Schumann added in conjunction with the Düsseldorf first performance of 1850 and with those corrections made by him presumably in this connection. Only within the Old Schumann Complete Edition did the *Adventlied* appear for the first time with trombone parts. Available up to that time were no other parts of this kind except those in the Düsseldorf *Musikverein*, and the autograph score was in Clara Schumann's possession. Hence, up to the appearance of the *Adventlied* in the Old Complete Edition, performances not under the auspices of the Düsseldorf *Musikverein* occurred without trombones, because the score copies offered for sale by Breitkopf & Härtel as well as the score edition of 1866 based on these did not contain the trombone parts. But since the work is fully complete only with the addition of the trombones, the New Schumann Complete Edition is based in the orchestral part on the autograph score and the extant orchestral parts containing the three trombone parts produced in 1850 by Friedrich Ottmann that have been consulted as comparison source.

Listed in the following individual comments are the essential differences between the sources mentioned. This is based on the Editorial Notes of volume VI/3/1,2 of the New Schumann Complete Edition.[10] Not mentioned are abbreviations or parallel passages that are not written out in the autograph score, as well as notational differences existing in KA that do not indicate any conceptual changes. Likewise not mentioned are the passages where the double stems of two wind or string parts are notated on a single stave and Schumann notated articulation and dynamic markings in the autograph score only once, as well as slurs in parallel motion, since it may be assumed that the markings apply to both parts. Also dispensed with are differences between the autograph score and the score copies.

Editorial additions are indicated by [ ] and broken lines (slur placement).

Ute Scholz
Translation: Margit L. McCorkle

---

[10] *Robert Schumann. Neue Ausgabe sämtlicher Werke*, Series IV, Work Group 3, Vol.1, 2, ed. Ute Bär (now Scholz) (Mainz, 2011).

VORWORT

Das in dieser Ausgabe vorgelegte und bis heute zu wenig bekannte *Adventlied* op. 71 auf einen Text von Friedrich Rückert komponierte Robert Schumann im November/Dezember 1848 in Dresden. Den Text notierte er laut eigenem Vermerk am 7. Februar 1848 als Nr. 48 in die von ihm und seiner Frau Clara 1839 begonnene handschriftliche Sammlung von Gedichten, die sich ihrer Meinung nach zur Komposition eigneten. Die Abschrift, dessen Anlass nur zu vermuten ist, erfolgte inmitten der Arbeit an seiner Oper *Genoveva* op. 81. Möglicherweise suchte Schumann nach Texten für neue, eigene Chorkompositionen, die er mit dem von ihm im Januar 1848 in Dresden gegründeten *Verein für Chorgesang* aufführen konnte. Der Vermerk „vielleicht motettenartig zu behandeln" unter dem Titel in der Gedichtabschrift lässt zumindest darauf schließen, dass Schumann ein geistliches Chorwerk beabsichtigte. Mit der Komposition des Werkes begann er aber erst neun Monate später am 25. November, dem Tag, an dem er sich erstmalig mit Rückerts *Makamen* beschäftigte und vermutlich den Text zu *Verzweifle nicht im Schmerzensthal* op. 93 in die Sammlung von Gedichtabschriften übertrug. Dabei war er auf die Abschrift des *Adventliedes* gestoßen und möglicherweise zur Komposition angeregt worden. Das Werk hatte er am 19. Dezember 1848 beendet. Dieses Datum notierte er am Ende der autographen Partitur: „Dresden, / den 19ten December 1848 / R. Schumann".

Im Zusammenhang mit der Textwahl des *Adventliedes* auf den noch heute in den Kirchengesangbüchern zu findenden Text *Dein König kommt niedern Hüllen* ist immer wieder über Schumanns Religiosität und sein Verhältnis zur Kirchenmusik reflektiert worden. Es handelt sich hier um ein Werk, das wohl religiös aber mehr politisch und vom aktuellen Tagesgeschehen motiviert worden ist, von der Sehnsucht nach Frieden und den Revolutionsjahren 1848/49. Beide Werke stellen, so Arnfried Edler

eine eigenartige Mischgattung zwischen geselligem, versteckt poltischem und religiösem Gesang dar. Mit dem *Adventlied* op. 71 [...] betrat Schumann zuerst jenen merkwürdigen Bereich zwischen den etablierten Gattungen, dessen Entstehung durch eine spezifische, gegenüber bestimmten Konfessionen, Liturgien und überhaupt konstituierten Glaubensorganisationen indifferente Religiosität dieser Zeit zu erklären ist[1].

Friedrich Rückerts *Adventlied* soll um 1820 entstanden sein. Es erschien erstmals 1834 in der Ausgabe der *Gesammelten Gedichte von Friedrich Rückert* im Verlag von Carl Heyder in Erlangen. Zwischen 1836 und 1840 erschienen vier weitere, nicht identische Auflagen dieser Ausgabe[2], in denen das *Adventlied* jeweils mit unverändertem Text abgedruckt worden ist. In ein Kirchengesangbuch wurde es erstmals 1841 in Württemberg aufgenommen.

Schumanns Handexemplar der ersten Ausgabe von 1843[3] sowie die Ausgabe von 1841 aus dem Verlag von Johann David Sauerländer sind bis auf den Unterschied in der 6. Strophe „Finsternis" statt „Finsterniß" mit den Texten der Heyder'schen Ausgaben identisch[4]. Da Schumann aber diese dreibändige Ausgabe der Gedichte Friedrich Rückerts aus dem Verlag von Johann David Sauerländer von 1843 laut Eintrag in seinem *Haushaltbuch* erst am 31. Mai 1849 erworben hat, scheidet sie ebenfalls als Textgrundlage aus. Es ist daher wahrscheinlich, dass die im Besitz des Ehepaares Schumann zum Zeitpunkt der Abschrift vorhandene zweite Auflage der *Gesammelten Gedichte von Friedrich Rückert* aus dem Verlag von Carl Heyder, die Robert laut autographem

---

[1] Arnfried Edler, *Robert Schumann und seine Zeit*, Laaber 1982, S. 228.
[2] Aufgrund unterschiedlicher Seitenzahlen der Ausgaben ist das *Adventlied* jeweils auf verschiedenen Seiten zu finden.
[3] Robert-Schumann-Haus Zwickau, Archiv-Nr.: *6095, 1–C1/A4.*
[4] Auch Schumann notierte in seiner Gedichtabschrift „Finsterniß".

Vermerk auf dem Vorsatzblatt 1837 seiner Frau geschenkt hatte[5], als Vorlage für die Abschrift diente.

Gegenüber der vermuteten Textvorlage weist Schumanns Abschrift mehrere Abweichungen auf. Drei grundsätzliche Änderungen nahm er dann in der autographen Partitur vor.[6]

Am 17. März 1849 bot Robert Schumann das *Adventlied* dem Verlag N. Simrock in Bonn zum Druck an. In seiner Antwort vom 29. März erklärte sich der Verlag zwar bereit, etwas von Schumanns Kompositionen zu drucken, lehnte aber dieses Werk sowie das *Konzertstück für vier Hörner* op. 86 ab. Daraufhin nahm Schumann bereits am 19. April mit dem Verlag Breitkopf & Härtel Kontakt wegen des Druckes von op. 71 auf, der am 26. April das neue Werk annahm. Am 2. Mai übersandte Schumann die Stimmen und den Klavierauszug des *Adventliedes* an den Verlag.

Den späteren, auf Rückert zurückgehenden Titel *Adventlied* sollte das Werk anfangs nicht erhalten. Diesbezüglich schrieb Schumann im Begleitbrief der Sendung erläuternd an Hermann Härtel:

„Adventlied", wie es Rückert selbst genannt, wollte ich es nicht nennen, weil dies an eine bestimmte Jahreszeit erinnert und die Aufführung des Stückes dadurch gewissermaßen an eine Zeit gebannt wäre. „Cantate" ist ein ziemlich verbrauchtes Wort – und so blieb mir nichts als das einfache: Geistliches Gedicht, womit Sie, wie ich wünsche, vielleicht einverstanden sein werden.[7]

Schumann ließ sich dann schließlich doch von Hermann Härtel überzeugen und gab dem Werk den heute bekannten Titel.

Die gedruckten Vokalstimmen erschienen im Juni 1849 – Schumann erhielt sie am 22. Juni – und der zweihändige Klavierauszug im November 1849. Die Partitur wurde zunächst als Verlagsabschrift vertrieben, worauf der Vermerk „Die Partitur ist in saubern Abschriften von der Verlagshandlung zu beziehen" auf dem gedruckten Klavierauszug hinweist. Im Druck lag sie erst postum im April 1866 vor.

Bereits zwei Monate nachdem Schumann die Komposition des *Adventliedes* beendet hatte, probte er das Werk am 21. Februar in dem 1848 von ihm gegründeten *Verein für Chorgesang*. Bis zu diesem Zeitpunkt müssen demzufolge auch die Singstimmen aus der autographen Partitur ausgeschrieben gewesen sein. Auch in den *Versammlungen* bis zum 17. April ist das *Adventlied* studiert worden, worüber Schumanns Eintragungen in seinem *Chornotizbuch*[8] Auskunft geben. Am 12. September probte er dann letztmalig das Werk im Dresdner Chorgesangverein. Aber auch Julius Rietz in Leipzig war an dem Werk interessiert und erarbeitete es mit der 1802 gegründeten Leipziger Singakademie. Am 10. Dezember 1849 wurde es dann unter seiner Leitung im *Konzert zum Besten der hiesigen Armen* im Gewandhaus durch die Leipziger Singakademie und den Thomanerchor uraufgeführt.

Bereits im Februar 1850 ist es in Schumanns Geburtsstadt Zwickau erstaufgeführt worden. Weitere, auf dem Vorsatzblatt von seinem Handexemplar des Klavierauszuges erwähnte Aufführungen fanden am 24. Oktober 1850 in Düsseldorf und am 12. Mai 1856 im Rahmen des 24. Niederrheinischen Musikfestes unter Julius Rietz statt[9].

---

[5] Robert-Schumann-Haus Zwickau, Archiv-Nr.: *7901–C1/A4*. Schumann notierte auf dem Vorsatzblatt: „Clara Schumann hat dies Buch geschenkt bekommen im J. 1837 von ihrem damaligen Liebsten Robert."

[6] Alle diese Unterschiede sind aufgelistet worden in: *Robert Schumann. Neue Ausgabe sämtlicher Werke*, Serie IV, Werkgruppe 3, Bd. 1, 2, hg. von Ute Bär (jetzt Scholz), Mainz 2011.

[7] Hessische Landes- und Hochschulbibliothek, Musikabteilung, Darmstadt; Breitkopf & Härtel Archiv, Signatur: *Nr. 69*. Die Abdrucke in *Robert Schumanns Briefe. Neue Folge*, hg. von F. Gustav Jansen, Leipzig 1886, S. 372f. und *Briefe NF, 2/1904*, S. 460f. sind unvollständig.

[8] Robert Schumann-Haus Zwickau, Archiv-Nr.: *4871 / VII,C, 6–A3*.

[9] Diesen Vermerk ergänzte Clara Schumann auf dem Vorsatzblatt von Schumanns Handexemplar.

Revisionsbericht

Überlieferte Notenquellen

SK   Skizzen zu op. 71
Universitäts- und Landesbibliothek
Bonn, Signatur: *Schumann 6*
Die zwischen dem 25. und 30. November 1848 in Dresden entstandenen Skizzen des *Adventliedes* wurden im November 1911 vom Oberbergrat Dr. h.c. Alfred Wiede in Leipzig bei C. G. Boerner zusammen mit zahlreichen anderen Autographen außer Katalog erworben. Das Manuskript befand sich bis 1974 im Besitz der Erben Alfred Wiedes und wurde dann durch das Musikantiquariat Hans Schneider, Tutzing, an die derzeitige Besitzerinstitution verkauft.
Das Manuskript umfasst drei, ursprünglich mit einem roten, heute offenen Bändchen verbundene Bogen gleichen Papiertyps à 4 Seiten, die jeweils mit 24 Systemen handschriftlich rastriert und nacheinander mit schwarzbrauner Tinte beschrieben worden sind.
Die Skizzen enthalten vornehmlich den Vokalsatz. Dabei hat Schumann ab der zweiten Seite die Notierung in Particellform aufgegeben und bis zur letzten Seite auf den jeweils vier Systeme umfassenden Akkoladen die einzelnen, nicht immer vollständig ausgeführten Vokalstimmen niedergeschrieben. Der Worttext ist (wenn auch nicht immer in allen Stimmen) vollständig vorhanden.

P   Autographe Partitur zu op. 71
Staatsbibliothek zu Berlin, Preußischer Kulturbesitz, Musikabteilung mit Mendelssohn-Archiv, Signatur *Mus. ms. autogr. R. Schumann 8*
Die zwischen dem 3. und 19. Dezember 1848 in Dresden entstandene und vor dem 22. Oktober 1850 in Düsseldorf ergänzte autographe Partitur, die mit den Autographen *Mus. ms. autogr. R. Schumann 9* (op. 93) und *Mus. ms. autogr. R. Schumann 10* (op. 144) zusammengebunden ist, wurde 1887 von Clara Schumann gemeinsam mit anderen Handschriften Robert Schumanns der Königlichen Bibliothek Berlin zum Kauf angeboten. Seit 1890 befand sie sich dort als Depositum. Durch die Finanzierung des Berliner Verlagsbuchhändlers Dr. Hermann Paetel ist es in den Besitz der heutigen Staatsbibliothek zu Berlin – Preußischer Kulturbesitz, übergegangen.
Die autographe Partitur des *Adventliedes* op. 71 umfasst 72 Seiten.
Dem Notentext ist ein nicht rastriertes Titelblatt vorangestellt, auf dessen recto-Seite Schumann in dunkelbrauner Tinte mittig den Werktitel notierte.
Der Notentext umfasst 17, jeweils mit 24 Systemen mit hellbrauner Tinte handrastrierte Bogen und ein Einzelblatt, auf denen Schumann fortlaufend den Notentext notiert hat.

OS   Originalausgabe der Singstimmen zu op. 71
Leipzig, bei Breitkopf & Härtel, Juni 1849
Titelblatt: *ADVENTLIED / von / Friedrich Rückert / für Sopran Solo und Chor / mit Begleitung des Orchesters / componirt / von / ROBERT SCHUMANN. / OP. 71. / Singstimmen. / Eigenthum der Verleger. / Leipzig, bei Breitkopf & Härtel. / Pr. 1 Thlr. / 7971. / Eingetragen in das Vereinsarchiv.*
OS umfasst die Stimmen von Sopran (einschließlich des Soloparts), Alt, Tenor I, Tenor II und Bass. Der Wechsel zwischen Solo und Chor

wird in den einzelnen Stimmen durch *Solo* bzw. *Chor* über dem jeweiligen System vermerkt. Bei gleichzeitigem Einsatz von Solo und Chor sind die Stimmen auf zwei getrennten Systemen gestochen worden.

KA   Originalausgabe des Klavierauszuges zu op. 71

Leipzig, bei Breitkopf & Härtel vermutlich zwischen dem 16. September und 16. Oktober 1849

Titelblatt: *Adventlied / von / Friedrich Rückert / für Sopran Solo und Chor / mit Begleitung des Orchesters / componirt / von / ROBERT SCHUMANN. / Op. 71. / Clavierauszug / VON R. PFRETZSCHNER. / Eigenthum der Verleger. / Leipzig, bei Breitkopf & Härtel. / Pr. 1 Thlr. 15 Ngr. / 7970. / Eingetragen in das Vereinsarchiv. / Die Partitur ist in saubern Abschriften von der Verlagshandlung zu beziehen.*

Der Notentext befindet sich auf den S. 3–35. Die verso-Seiten des Titelblattes und des letzten Notenblattes sind leer.

HAD   Handschriftliche Aufführungsstimmen des Städtischen Musikvereins Düsseldorf zu op. 71

Heinrich-Heine-Institut Düsseldorf; *Depositum des Städtischen Musikvereins Düsseldorf*, Nr.: *367.3*

Das vor dem 24. Oktober 1850 und dem 12. Mai 1856 vom *Adventlied* angefertigte Aufführungsmaterial des Düsseldorfer Musikvereins umfasst neben gedruckten Vokal- und Streichquartettstimmen 35 handschriftliche Orchester- und 46 Vokalstimmen. Die Instrumentalstimmen sind größtenteils von Otto Hermann Klausnitz geschrieben und für die Aufführung im Rahmen des Niederrheinischen Musikfestes 1856 angefertigt worden. Daneben enthält das Konvolut fünf von A. Ottmann notierte Instrumentalstimmen, die wohl im Zusammenhang mit der Düsseldorfer Erstaufführung des Werkes am 24. Oktober 1851 angefertigt worden sind. Unter den von Ottmann geschriebenen befinden sich alle drei Posaunenstimmen, die Korrekturen aufweisen, die mit denen im Partiturautograph übereinstimmen und möglicherweise aufführungsbedingt sind.

PA 1–3   Partiturabschriften 1–3 zu op. 71

PA 1   Gesellschaft der Musikfreunde in Wien; Signatur: *28159*

PA 2   Toonkunst-Bibliothek, Amsterdam; Signatur: *Mus. Schum 2*

PA 3   Toonkunst-Bibliothek, Amsterdam; Signatur: *Mus. Schum 3*

Nachdem Schumann am 2. Dezember 1849 die Korrekturfahne der Vorlage für die Verkaufsabschriften der Partitur an Breitkopf und Härtel zurückgeschickt hatte, konnten die auf dem Titelblatt des Klavierauszuges KA angekündigten Partituren angefertigt und vertrieben werden. Zu diesem Zeitpunkt hatte Schumann die Posaunenstimmen noch nicht ergänzt, so dass die entsprechenden Abschriften diese nicht enthalten konnten.

Die von verschiedenen Kopisten geschriebenen Partituren PA 1 und PA 2 umfassen jeweils 76 Seiten und weisen die gleiche Takt- und Systemaufteilung sowie den gleichen Titel auf der ersten Notenseite über dem ersten System auf. Möglich ist daher, dass sie von der gleichen Vorlage abgeschrieben worden sind. Deutliche Unterschiede zu diesen beiden Abschriften weist die Partiturabschrift PA 3 auf.

EST   Erstausgabe der Streichquartettstimmen zu op. 71

Leipzig, bei Breitkopf & Härtel,

Mai 1856

Kopftitel: *ADVENTLIED / von / ROBERT SCHUMANN / Op. 71 / Leipzig bei Breitkopf & Härtel.* Unter dem Kopftitel ist die jeweilige Stimmenangabe (*Violino I., Violino II., Viola., Violoncello e Basso.*) gestochen worden. Die Plattennummer *9319* befindet sich auf jeder Notenseite. Auf der ersten Notenseite der Vl. I-Stimme ist unten links der Vermerk: *Stich und Druck von Breitkopf & Härtel in Leipzig.* gestochen worden.

Die Stimmen von Vl. I, Vl. II und Vla. umfassen jeweils vier, die von Vc./Cb. fünf Notenseiten.

EP Erstausgabe der Partitur zu op. 71 Leipzig, bei Breitkopf & Härtel, April 1866

Kopftitel: *ADVENTLIED / von / ROBERT SCHUMANN / für Sopran Solo und Chor / mit Begleitung des Orchesters / componirt / von / ROBERT SCHUMANN / Op. 71. / PARTITUR. / Eigenthum der Verleger. / Leipzig, bei Breitkopf & Härtel. / Pr. 3 Thlr. 15 Ngr. / 10818. / Eingetragen in das Vereinsarchiv.*

In der postum erschienenen Erstausgabe der Partitur fehlen ebenso wie in den überlieferten Partiturabschriften die Posaunenstimmen. Ansonsten weist sie ebenso wie die Partiturabschriften gegenüber der autographen Partitur keine konzeptionellen Unterschiede auf.

Quellenbewertung und Edition

Die Werkgenese ist beim *Adventlied* durch die heute überlieferten und vom Komponisten autorisierten Dokumente nicht vollständig belegt. Erhalten sind zum einen die Quellen, die frühe Textstadien dokumentieren, zum anderen sind die vom Komponisten überwachten Originalausgaben der Singstimmen und des Klavierauszuges, die wiederum gegenüber der autographen Partitur Varianten enthalten, sowie die für die Düsseldorfer Erstaufführung benutzten handschriftlichen Posaunenstimmen überliefert. Verschollen sind all jene Quellen, die die Textstufen zwischen der autographen Partitur und den 1849 erschienenen Originalausgaben der Singstimmen und des Klavierauszugs dokumentieren. Hierzu gehören der vor dem 20. Februar 1849 von Robert Pfretzschner erstellte handschriftliche Klavierauszug, die vor dem 21. Februar gefertigten handschriftlichen Singstimmen, die Schumann bis zum Erscheinen der Originalausgabe und eventuell auch darüber hinaus noch im Dresdner Chorgesangverein benutzte, sowie die Stichvorlagen und die Korrekturfahnen für die Originalausgaben der Singstimmen und des Klavierauszuges. Nicht überliefert ist weiterhin die von Schumann durchgesehene Stammabschrift für die Verlagsabschriften der Partitur, die vermutlich als Vorlage für die ebenfalls verschollenen handschriftlichen Orchesterstimmen der Leipziger Uraufführung diente.

Aus dieser Quellenüberlieferung wird deutlich, dass für die Singstimmen und den Klavierauszug deren Originalausgaben und – da die Streichquartettstimmen erst im Mai 1856 und die Partitur 1866 im Druck vorlagen – für die Orchesterstimmen die autographe Partitur die jeweiligen Hauptquellen bilden. Als Vergleichsquelle für die Singstimmen diente die Originalausgabe des Klavierauszuges.

Der Orchesterpart wird in der revidierten Endfassung mit Posaunen, die Schumann im Zusammenhang mit der Düsseldorfer Erstaufführung von 1850 hinzugefügt hat und den von ihm vermutlich im diesem Zusammenhang vorgenommenen Korrekturen, ediert. Erst im Rahmen der Alten Schumann-Gesamtausgabe erschien das *Adventlied* erstmals mit Posaunenstimmen. Bis zu diesem Zeitpunkt lagen außer im Düsseldorfer Musikverein keine weiteren derartigen Stimmen vor, und die autographe Partitur befand sich im Besitz Clara Schumanns. Somit sind bis zum Erscheinen des *Adventliedes* in der Alten Gesamtausgabe nicht vom Düsseldorfer Musikverein verantwortete Aufführungen ohne Posaunen erfolgt, denn die vom Verlag Breitkopf & Härtel vertriebenen Partiturabschriften enthielten ebenso wie der Partiturdruck von 1866 diese nicht. Da das Werk aber erst mit der Hinzufügung der Posaunen vollständig und fertig geworden ist, basiert die Neue Schumann-Gesamtausgabe und damit auch die vorliegende im Orchesterpart auf der autographen Partitur und den 1850 von Friedrich Ottmann gefertigten, die drei Posaunenstimmen enthaltenden Orchesterstimmen, die als Vergleichsquelle herangezogen worden sind.

In den folgenden Einzelanmerkungen werden die wesentlichen Unterschiede zwischen den benannten Quellen aufgelistet. Diese basieren auf dem Revisionsbericht des Bandes VI/3/1,2 der Neuen Schumann-Gesamtausgabe[10]. Nicht erwähnt werden in der autographen Partitur nicht ausgeschriebene Abbreviaturen oder Parallelstellen sowie auch im KA vorhandene Notationsunterschiede, die keine konzeptionellen Änderungen bedeuten. Ebenfalls nicht erwähnt werden die Passagen, bei denen Schumann in der autographen Partitur bei Doppelbehalsung von zwei auf einem System notierten Bläser- oder Streicherstimmen Artikulations- und dynamische Zeichen sowie Bögen bei Parallelführung nur einmal notierte, da davon auszugehen ist, dass die Angaben für beide Stimmen gelten sollen. Verzichtet wird auch auf die zwischen der autographen Partitur und den Partiturabschriften vorhandenen Abweichungen.

Ergänzungen der Herausgeberin werden im Notentext durch [ ] bzw. Strichelungen (Bogenetzung) kenntlich gemacht.

Ute Scholz

---

[10] *Robert Schumann. Neue Ausgabe sämtlicher Werke,* Serie IV, Werkgruppe 3, Bd. 1, 2, hg. von Ute Bär (jetzt Scholz), Mainz 2011.

Textual Notes

Bar	Stave	Source	Comments
2	Fl. 1, 2	P	Because the original b2 is cancelled, connecting slur from b1 is lacking
3–4	V.-Hn. 1	P	Slur notated to b3, 2nd ♩, connecting slur to b4 lacking, in b4 connecting slur is present (system break)
6–9	Fl. 2; Hob. 2	P	Only ties notated.
8–9	Fl. 1, 2; Hob. 1; Clar. 1; Vl. I; Br.	P	Slur drawn over the barline, after the page turn slur in b9 begins with 1st note, connecting slur lacking. Assumed is that Schumann had planned a connecting slur.
9–10	Fg. 1	P	Only tie notated.
	Fg. 2	P	Slur to b10, 1st beat; adjusted in the edition to the other parts
14–23	Br.	P	Single and double stems notated inconsistently. Assumed is that Schumann planned parts division up to b23 (last double-stemmed bar).
16	Choir, Alto	KA	*Empfang'* instead of *empfang'*
18	Solo, Soprano	OS	*cresc.* to 5th beat for space reasons
		KA	*cresc.* engraved between 4th and 5th beats; based in the edition on the Br. part as in P, where *cresc.* has been notated only once between Br. and Solo Soprano, notated to 4th beat
20	Orchestral parts	P	< > varying in all parts, partly notated as ◁— —▷
*24	Hob. 2; Clar. 2	P	Slurs in Hob. 2 and Clar. 2, 4th –5th beats lacking. Not excluded is that Schumann intended a phrasing suitable to the first part
	V.-Hn. 1, 2	P	*muta in E* lacking, b33 notated *in E*.
28–30	Fl. 2; Hob. 2; Clar 2	P	Legato slurs lacking.
29	W.-Hn. 1, 2; V.-Tr. 1, 2		*muta in E* lacking, b33 notated *in E*.
32	Solo Soprano	KA	Full stop instead of comma after *angenehm*
32–33	Fl. 2	P	Only tie to b33 e^2-e^2 notated

41–43	Kl.-A.	KA	♫ -appoggiaturas instead of ♪♪ -appoggiaturas in Vc./Cb. adopted in the edition, since not excluded is that this change was intended.
48–49	Tenor, Bass	KA	*O Mächtiger*
53	Soprano, Alto	KA	Full stop instead of *!*
69	Bass	OS	*cresc.* notated to 3rd beat; the edition follows KA based on the notation in other parts and in comparison with P
	Kl.-A.	KA	*cresc.* engraved to 3rd beat; corrected in the edition based on the notation in the parts
71	Tenor I	OS	Comma instead of full stop
	Tenor II	OS	; instead of full stop
73–75	Kl.-A.	P, KA	Compared with P differing slur placement adopted in the edition
77	W.-Hn. 1, 2	P	*muta in G* lacking, b96 notated *in G* above the stave
78	Soprano	OS	Comma after *gründest* lacking
79	V.-Tr. 1, 2	P	*muta in D* lacking, b101 *in D* notated above the stave
	Pk.	P	*muta in d/G* lacking, b102 *in d/G* notated above the stave
80	Fl. 1	P	Slur notated up to b81, 1st beat a²; corrected in the edition because of the pitch repetition.
	Kl.-A.	KA	< > as ⟨ ⟩ 1st–4th beat; adjusted in the edition to the orchestral parts
82	V.-Hn. 1, 2	P	*muta in D* lacking, b92 *in D* notated above the stave
90–99	Fg. 1	P	Slurs lacking, comment *legato* b89; slurs added in the edition after the parallel-motion Br. part
95	Clar. 1	P	Slur to 1st –4th beat. Corrected in the edition because of the pitch repetition.
	Kl.-A.	KA	Slur revised corresponding to the corrections in the parts
97	Tenor I	OS	Last word *den* instead of *der*
100	Bass	OS	*cresc.* notated between 1st and 2nd notes; the edition follows KA also based on P

101–103	Fg. 1		Slur lacking. Not excluded is that Schumann intended a suitable phrasing for the second part.
102	Vl. I	P	Second quaver originally f, slur thus presumably beginning with 1st quaver
	Vl. II	P	Slur for 1st–2nd beats presumably from original variant e1–d1
105	Tenor I, II	KA	Full stop after *hinaus* and subsequent capitalization of *Bewaffnet-*
106	Clar. 1	P	Slur beginning with 1st note
	Pk.	P	3rd–4th beats notated as crotchet with tie
106–108	Fl. 2; Hob. 2; Clar. 2		Only ties notated. Not excluded is that Schumann also intended a suitable phrasing of the first part.
111	Fg.; Cb.; Kl.-A.	P	3rd–4th beats: slur variously notated; adjusted in the edition to other woodwind parts
114	Soprano	KA	Full stop engraved after *Bahn*
116	Pos. 1	P	*mf* notated
		HAD	*mf* adopted from P, corrected to *f*
123	Pk.	P	3rd–4th beats: A notated; corrected in the edition corresponding to the tuning in d/G
125	Pos. 1	HAD	4th beat originally notated as f sharp1, corrected in final variant documented in P and *f* added corresponding to P
134–135	Soprano; Alto; Tenor I	KA	⟩ engraved to the end of b134
135	Hob. 1, 2; Br.	P	⟩ notated to the end of b134
147	Kl.-A., KA upper stave		Slur beginning with f1; adjusted in the edition to Vl. I
148	Kl.-A.		Slur added corresponding to the correction in Vc.
150	Solo Soprano Kl.-A., KA upper stave	KA	Comma lacking after *stiften* ⟨ b149, beginning 4th beat; adjusted in the edition to the orchestral parts

168	Clar. 1, 2	P	c¹ not stemmed, d¹ notated stemmed upward; the edition follows the reading notated in the score copy
173	V.-Hn. 1, 2	P	*muta in D* lacking, b177 notated *in D* above the stave and b179 *2 Ventil Hörner in D.* notated before the stave
175	Kl.-A.	KA	*dimin* notated between ♩ and ♪; adjusted in the edition to the orchestral parts
184	Tenor 2	OS	1ˢᵗ beat: *p* engraved; the edition follows KA based on the other parts, although not excluded is that present is a correction intended by Schumann.
190	Soprano	OS	*o* instead of *O*. The edition follows KA based on the previous punctuation.
195–196	Bass	OS	Comma and *o* instead of *!* and *O*; the edition follows KA based on the notation in the other parts
199	Bass	KA	*!* and *O* instead of comma and *o*; the edition follows OS based on the other parts
201	Soprano	OS	*!* instead of comma; the edition follows KA based on the other parts
204	Clar. 2, Fg. 1	P	< > lacking
	Kl.-A.	KA	3ʳᵈ beat: < > as ◁── ──▷ for 1ˢᵗ–4ᵗʰ beats
217	Kl.-A.	KA	Comma after *kommst* lacking
228	Vl. I	P	*cresc.* to the 3ʳᵈ beat of originally notated, cancelled variant
	Vc.	P	added *cresc.* between 2ⁿᵈ and 3ʳᵈ beats
230–233	Fl. 2; Hob. 2; Clar. 2; Fg. 2	P	Slurs lacking. Not excluded is that Schumann intended a suitable phrasing of the first part also in the second part.

236–243	Fg.	P	Bars 236, 3rd beat–238, 4th beat, slur for Fg. 2 notated, slur for Fg. 1 lacking. Bar 239 comment *a2*, slur placed above the stave up to b242. Slur placement in the edition adjusted to the other parts.
237	Kl.-A., upper stave	KA	*sf* engraved above the stave; notated in the edition taking lower stemming of the score into account
238–242	Hob. 1	P	Slur lacking. Not excluded is that Schumann intended a suitable phrasing of the second part also in Hob. 1
	Hob. 2	P	Slur beginning with the 1st beat in b238; slur new beginning, b239 (page turn); corrected in the edition because of the pitch repetition
238	Kl.-A., upper stave	KA	4th beat: 1st quaver a¹ engraved with upward stemming; corrected in the edition from Vl. II
243	Fl. 2	P	Slur notated 3rd beat to the end of the bar, connecting slur to b244 lacking; cancelled in the edition because of the subsequent course of the part
246–247	Vc.	P	Notated in 𝄢
249–250	Pos. 1	HAD	Connecting slur to b250 adopted from P, later corrected in the variant adopted in the edition
253–255	Pos. 1	P	Only tie notated, legato slur lacking; notated in the edition from HAD, where the legato slur has been added to the end of the bar
253–254	Pos. 3	P	Slur ending between 2 ♩ and barline; the edition follows HAD
258–260	Pos. 2	P	Slur lacking; the edition follows HAD
	Pos. 3	P	Slur notated to the end of b258 (page turn); the edition follows HAD
260	Pk.	P	*muta in d/G* lacking; b266 notated *in G, D*

265	Orchestral parts	P	*cresc.* notated between 2nd and 3rd beats
	Choral parts	OS	*cresc.* notated in the Soprano and Alto always for ♩ 1st–2nd beats, in Tenor I, II and Bass for the 3rd beat
		KA	*cresc.* always notated for the 3rd beat; adopted in the edition from P
273	Solo Tenor; Solo Bass	KA	3rd–4th beats not notated
274	Pos. 1–3	P	Comment *3 Posaunen ad libitum* before b274
278	Choral parts	OS	*cresc.* notated in Tenor II and Bass for the 1st note, in Soprano and Alto between 1st and 2nd notes, in Tenor II for the 2nd note
		KA	*cresc.* notated in all parts for the 1st note; placed on the 2nd note in the edition also based on the orchestral parts as in P
280	Vocal parts; Kl.-A.	OS, KA	*cresc.* notated except in the Alto (OS) always on the 3rd beat; notated in the edition based on the orchestral parts as in P
291	Tenor I	OS, KA	Comma instead of *!*; adjusted in the edition to the other parts
295	Alto	OS	*cresc.* engraved for the 2nd beat, 2nd quaver
	Kl.-A., KA upper stave		2nd beat: engraved ⁊ added in the upward stemming
299	Fl. 1		Parallel motion not written out in the Soprano; the accent present there adopted in the edition adjusted to the other wind parts.
306	Pos. 1	HAD	Notated originally as f sharp¹, corrected in variant documented in P to d sharp¹ and the letter *dis* added below the stave
307–310	Pos. 1, 2	HAD	Slur notated to the end of b309. Since no kind of correction is extant, the edition follows P in which the slur has been carried on to b310.

309–310	Fg. 1	P	Slurs lacking. Not excluded is that Schumann intended a phrasing suitable for the second part.
311	Pos. 3	P	Slur notated to the end of b310; the edition follows HAD
312–313	Fg. 2	P	Slur lacking. Not excluded is that Schumann intended a phrasing suitable for the first part.
315	Tenor	KA	♮ for c^1 lacking
326	Pos. 1	HAD	Last crotchet originally notated g^1, finally corrected to the variant b^1 documented in P
332	Fl. 1; Hob. 2	P	Parallel motion with the Soprano not written out; there the lacking slur added in the edition adjusted to Clar. 1
333	Fl. 1, 2; Hob. 1, 2	P	notated
	Pos.1–3	P	beginning between 1st and 2nd ♩
		HAD	always beginning with 1st ♩
	Soprano, Bass	OS	engraved b334; the edition follows also based on P and the other parts KA
	Kl.-A.	KA	beginning with the 2nd beat; adjusted to the orchestral parts
339–340	Fl. 1, 2; Hob. 1, 2		Parallel motion with the Soprano and Alto not written out; the accents present there adjusted to the Clar. 1, 2 and Fg. 1, 2 are not adopted in the edition
358	Orchestral parts	P	*cresc.* inconsistent, but mostly notated in the middle of the bar; adjusted in the edition to the notation in vocal parts
		HAD	*cresc.* in Pos.1, 2 at the beginning of the bar, notated in Pos. b357
	Kl.-A.	KA	*cresc.* engraved on the 4th beat; adjusted in the edition to the orchestral parts
362	Fl. 1		In the present text slur Soprano text adjusted to Hob. 2 not adopted in the edition

	Kl.-A.	KA	*ff* engraved; adjusted in the edition to the orchestral parts
369	Fl. 1, 2	P	Parallel motion with the Soprano and Alto not written out; the *p* present not adopted from the Soprano and Alto, since it was already notated in b368
373	Tenor I	OS	*!* instead of comma; the edition follows KA based on Tenor II
385	Solo parts	KA	Comma instead of *!* and *o* instead of *O*
	Choral parts	KA	Full stop instead of *!*
386	Solo Soprano	OS	*o* instead of *O*; adjusted in the edition to the other parts
389	Vc.; Cb.	P	*sfz* notated; adjusted in the edition to the other parts

ADVENTLIED

Robert Schumann
(1810–1856)
Op. 71

*) In T. 212–254, T. 260–275 sowie T. 375–591 erfolgt zusätzlich der Einsatz von Chor-Soli. / In addition, choral soloists are specified in bb212–35, 260–73, and 375–91.

Edited by Ute Scholz
© 2012 Ernst Eulenburg Ltd, London
and Ernst Eulenburg & Co GmbH, Mainz

2

Kö - nig kommt in nie - dern Hül - len, ihn trägt der last - bar'n Es' - lin Fül - len, em - pfang' ihn

8

No. 2 **Die Viertel etwas langsamer wie vorher**

10

14

18

26

30

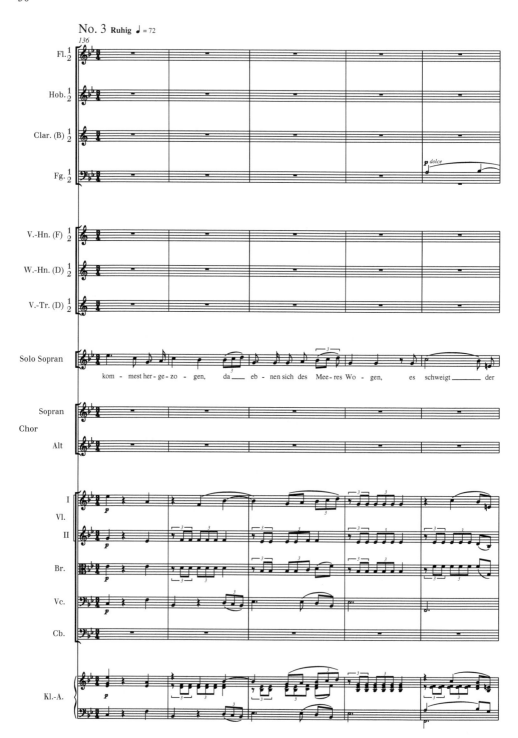

No. 3 Ruhig ♩ = 72

kom - mest her - ge - zo - gen, da___ eb - nen sich des Mee - res Wo - gen, es schweigt____ der

Sturm, von dir be-droht, es schweigt der Sturm. Du

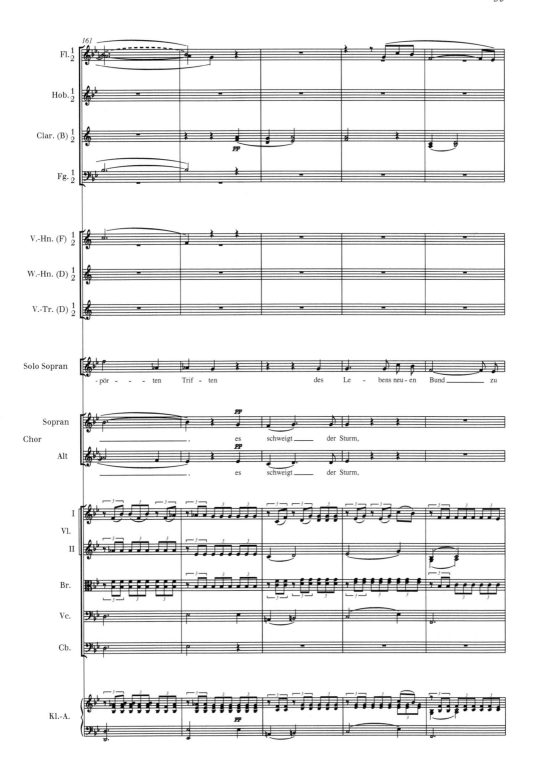

No. 4

44

No. 5 Etwas lebhafter

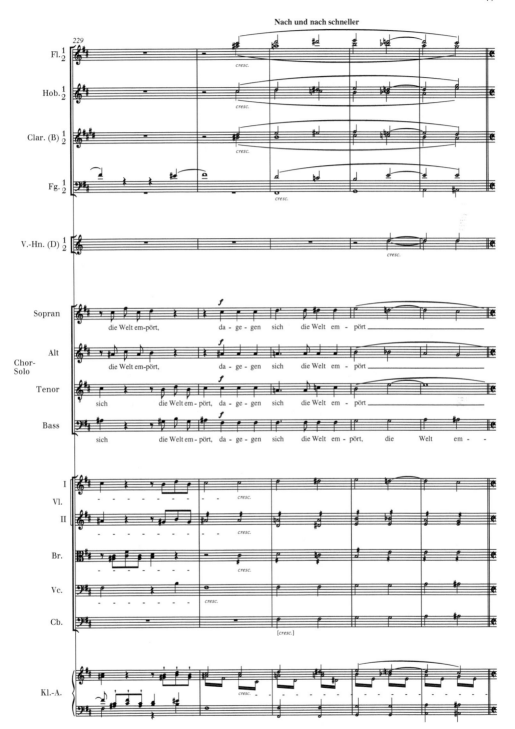

48

52

No. 7 Die Viertel etwas schneller wie vorher die Halben

70